Sold Love

Love Is All Around Us

Debanjali Nag

Ukiyoto Publishing

All global publishing rights are held by

Ukiyoto Publishing

Published in 2023

Content Copyright © Debanjali Nag

ISBN 9789360491529

All rights reserved.
No part of this publication may be reproduced, transmitted, or stored in a retrieval system, in any form by any means, electronic, mechanical, photocopying, recording or otherwise, without the prior permission of the publisher.

The moral rights of the authors have been asserted.

This is a work of fiction. Names, characters, businesses, places, events, locales, and incidents are either the products of the author's imagination or used in a fictitious manner. Any resemblance to actual persons, living or dead, or actual events is purely coincidental.

This book is sold subject to the condition that it shall not by way of trade or otherwise, be lent, resold, hired out or otherwise circulated, without the publisher's prior consent, in any form of binding or cover other than that in which it is published.

www.ukiyoto.com

Dedication

I dedicate this book to all the single mothers and single women who did rise back from the ashes after being broken into multiple fragments by their partners. Their life did not end there but some found love again while some found love in themselves for the rest of their life.

Contents

Love Happens In Pieces	17
See Through The Agony	18
The Heart And Soul Merges To Find The Betrayal	21
A Pinch In The Soul	22
Bitter Taste Of Love	25
The Roller Coaster Ride	26
Masks That Cover The Heart	29
A Musk So Clear	30
Springing Love For Another Time	33
Love Hails From West	34
Love Is Warm	38
A Love To Be Loved	39
Heavens Drool For The Heart	43
Love Is Like A Poem	44
About the Author	*48*

Dark Soul of the Knight

Between the tapestry of London streets and pulsing veins of Berlin,

Lived a man, coarse in ways of heart, though pleasant in his grin.

In a realm adorned with amber, cradled in East's tranquil lair,

Breathed a woman, softly radiating love, an aura uniquely rare.

Two entities separated by oceans, encompassed in divergent cities,

Twisted by fate's enchanting hand in an epic saga of realities.

She held the seat of innocence in Delhi's blossoming flowers,

He danced to an ethereal tune on Berlin's echoing towers.

Virtually their destinies danced, a moonlit masquerade of love,

Seducing dawn's purity with twilight's final, gentle shove.

She gave herself, unveiled and bare, surrendering her guarded trust,

Beneath the shimmering Indian skies and the cities laden with dust.

Only to find his shadows slithering, cloaked in his charming ways,

Between the spectre of grandeur and Berlin's smokey haze.

A lone act of physical release, claiming night as the intimate cover,

Torn open, the rifts of hearts, each vulnerability he did discover.

A serpent's sting dipped in sweetest poison, that's how he dared to strike,

And this, fair creatures, the age-old dance of love's cruel deceptive hike.

Her Eden lost to his serpent's tongue, their affections twisted and riled,

Their symphony lost in cacophony, the dirge of the innocent beguiled.

His deceitfulness etched in verses of pain, on her pristine love's tomb,

A wild blizzard brewed from a feigned whisper, heaved a never-ending gloom.

An ethereal glow her soul had possessed, tarnished by his vile action,

Crushed beneath Berlin's brutal skies, etched with irremovable faction.

Each letter, each word of apology scribed, dipped in frosty aloof disdain,

Flowed freely across her bruised heart's scroll, reinforcing her tormenting chain.

His actions stark, exhibiting his narcissistic traits, relentless and uncaring,

She learned of hearts too cruel to comprehend, her love's fabric quickly tearing.

From the grungy alleyways of Berlin to the adorned gates of Delhi,

The sweet melody of trust destroyed, a romanticism so smelly.

Twain met in passion's violent storm, with heartache the spoils of their weather,

Her innocence pilfered in stolen whispers, two souls untethered forever.

And so, it was in diverse cities, their tragic opera sung,

Echoing the halls of heartbreak where oft their hopes had hung.

On the precipice of trust and love, 'twas indeed a shattering sight,

Two strangers bound by an ugly break, vanquishing love's radiant light.

In the vestiges of dusk, I weave an elegy for hearts' brawls,

Strangers in birth, yet linked in a narrative which enthralls.

A man and woman played lovers in the summer haze,

But came the tempest, an embittered gloaming replaced blissful days.

Where there were lovers, lie broken shells, yearning answers unknown,

Of deeds unseen, of whispered tales the winds have sown.

Why must love become a transient haze, a lament sung so bitter?

From fires of passion and promise of dawn, to ashes so terribly litter.

With hush of silence came an unyielding distance,

A potent vacuum echoed across their shared existence.

The man ceased to commune, yet left his seed inside,

Her rounded womb carried more than a child; 'twas an estrangement magnified.

Where lies the error, ponders she in empty corners of twilight,

In her faithful amour, in trusting or seeking his sweet respite?

Did she commit to bear the lion's share, forsaking all prudence,

Or were his vain manners her ardent love's indulgence?

Yet amongst such fractured lament, there echoes no retaliation,

But silent acceptance of a tragically woven situation.

Upon their split, seeds of irony fell, revealing an allegory strange,

That love conceived in narcissistic laps, spawns no veritable change.

Her countenance transformed with grief and glory as the moon does in its phase,

While his echoing absence only revealed his self-indulgent craze.

His regard turned sour, apathy etched lines of distance and disdain,

Yet the impending fruit of their dissolved love is what she chooses to sustain.

Oh! How unfair the Cupid plays, dealing hands that challenge fates,

Two strangers who once sought solace, split in deplorable states.

Left to traverse a path born from loving recklessly wild,

Her crimson life absorbed into bearing the consequences, along with their child.

In the chaos of scattered sentiments, sprouted poetry of desolation,

An echo of affection reduced to icy withdrawal and intimidation.

A celestial waltz marred by conceit, guided by elusive constellation,

But she dares to hope, in her tender heart finds a mystical formation.

This cruel turn of celestial course is the ballad she must scribe,

The poem etched with her spirit's quill, life's daunting tale transcribed.

Yet among her pregnant laments and mirrored moonlit gaze,

Love abides not lost but transforms, shining in hope's comforting blaze.

Two strangers intertwined, bearing fruits of unripe love,

Within her breathes a testament of a tale penned above.

For he might turn away, enticed by his ego's narcotic wine,

But she bravely soldiers on, shaping their fate's fractured line.

Let these words bear the weight of this rueful narration,

In which love bloomed, then wilted under narcissism's deadly radiation.

Strangers, once heart-touched, to walk separate paths henceforth,

Sold Love

A mournful testimony of love's uncanny transformative worth.

Bleak yet infused with a beauty irrevocably marred,

This poem concludes on an eerie note, slightly charred.

For she bore the cost, his vanity turned their bond into specters,

Beware, my dear readers, of love between two woeful strangers.

From days of laughter and moments painted in hues,

Of holding hands beneath the watchful midnight blues,

They lived a dream, one heart under their chests,

The union of two strangers, sharing each other's nests.

Their story wasn't filled with petals or love's reign,

His eyes reflecting a rainbow after much-needed rain.

With charm came deceit, masked by alluring grin,

Behind his affection lay his narcissistic kin.

He basked in vanity, conceited was his art,

Slowly with each blow, breaking her innocent heart.

Where once there was love, resentment took its place,

An ominous shroud upon the glow of her grace.

What wrong had she done? She couldn't comprehend,
For all she had done was love without pretend.
In his game of illusion, she was but a pawn,
Stranded, betrayed, desolated at the break of dawn.
In her womb, a new life was budding,
Yet the news brought more than a heart thudding.
Losing herself in pain, in life's tempestuous sea,
Unspoken truths swelled within her quietly.
Parents ought to be refuge in such an awful storm,
But in their wrath, a daughter's love was torn.
A child by herself, pregnant, rejected,
In her heart, the wounds silently reflected.
Life now held a twist, as tales often weave,
In pain and loneliness, she chose to believe.
Working her hours under the judging stare,
In strength, she wore motherhood with such rare flair.
Though despair wore heavy, her spirits couldn't bend,
With each night, towards life, she learnt to mend.
On lonely evenings when she crooned lullabies,
Tales of their past fell from her tired eyes.

What's love if not a rogue, mischievous and spry?
Brewing tales of passion beneath the moon's sly eye.
With love came torment, yet with pain she thrived,
Taming her scars, in love's absence, she survived.
Though theirs was a story of love gone astray,
In her strength, a new saga paved its way.
Between two strangers, in the echo of goodbyes,
The whispering truth of love, life defies.
For life isn't just blossoms of youthful glee,
In fragments, it holds love's forgotten spree.
In her silence, in her tears, a resolve arose,
The heroine of her tale, in pain's prose.
Broken yet hopeful, weary yet willing,
In her lone dance with life, she found it thrilling.
From an uncertain love to an unwavering stride,
Her tale wove resilience, no storm could hide.
And thus the dance of two strangers finds its end,
Yet within the woman, a phoenix starts to ascend.
Love may have fled, left scars on her path,
But within the wound, blooms strength's loving bath.

Such is the journey of love's tired travelers,
Through pains and partings, love's skilled weavers.
While some are gifted an endless sunny day,
Others find their love in the moon's gray.
As long as hearts endure, as long as hearts do break,
Love shall weave its tale, for a soul's humble sake.
Even as tears trickle down from sky's watery eyes,
A tale of resilience shall beneath its veil rise.
She held her world within her arms, tiny yet vast,
A lullaby the soundtrack to her days long past.
Hoping love would lift her burdened heart, restore,
The dream of a family, crushed in silence so raw.
Bitter remembrance of the charmer who smiled,

His treacherous ways concealed, her innocence beguiled.
Left with naught but echoes of laughter turned disdain,
Wondering, she reflected upon what misdeed held her chain.
Pillars of society peered from high, echoing in fright,

Casting doubt upon her resilience, to undermine her fight.

The child is best elsewhere, whispers turned into a din,

Unfazed, she whispered back, In love, my strength, I find within.

Frugality became her solace, each penny counted thrice,

Labouring day and night, with hopes to pay the price.

To cross the boundless oceans, to reach another shore,

Where past sorrows would be shadows, reminders no more.

In pursuit of that foreign land, two jobs she would dare,

Nurturing the sprouting life, tucked within her care.

Not a helping hand extended, childhood friends had flown,

Yet she toiled and thrived, adamant, proud and alone.

Till came the day, with a small suitcase, filled with dreams she held dear,

Her land of hope awaited, as the final farewells drew near.

Venturing into unknown realms, the brave woman took a flight,

Holding tight her tiny bundle, glistening under the moonlight.

In her baby's eyes, she saw a brighter day, a future formed anew,

She wiped away her salty tears, as their old world they outgrew.

Stepping onto unfamiliar ground, holding hope within her palm,

A new dawn had arrived, she was no more, the woman unsure, and calm.

Heartbreaks she endured, disappointments plenty and losses she had seen,

Yet her strength lay unfathomable, in places others hadn't been.

Anonymity was their cloak, under which they grew in might,

Two strangers forging an odyssey, against the relentless night.

An epitome of fortitude, mother and child strode on,

A bond stronger than pain, stronger than a tale gone wrong.

Broken but undeterred, in each other they found solace,

From love lost, a new love sprung, beating the odds in place.

Their tale lingers still, a song whispered with pride,

In the hush of moonlit lullabies, across the oceans wide.

Speak not of the heart that was wronged, speak instead of courage pure,

Two strangers turned warriors, a testament to love's cure.

The twilight whispered their parting tales,

Upon an enchanted eve of regret and pain.

With passion dimmed and love turned pale,

Two hearts diverged ne'er to meet again.

From doting eyes she slipped away,

Clad in courage, donned in deceit,

Under the cover of shadowed gray,

She hid a secret, bittersweet.

With tiny heart against her own,

A reminder of their long-lost flame.

A solitary song of love unknown,
Born from pain, yet void of blame.
Years turned seasons in their dance,
Silent, unforgotten chance.
Two paths converge, oh bitter strife!
Awakening a sleeping slice of life.
Shimmering tears in his knowing eyes,
A specter of past, an unexpected surprise,
A progeny sprung from an unborn star,
Stirring echoes of a love from afar.
Upon this revelation harsh and real,
The old wounds gaped, refused to heal.
Their entangled destiny lured him back,
Across the trail of their faded track.
A whispered prayer, a plea to fight,
Within the realm of wrong and right.
A tale of love twisted and torn,
In the shadow of the vows they'd sworn.
He pleaded union under the sovereign sky,
A request, she chose, to deny.

She battled fierce in the halls of law,
For her child, her world, and the love she saw.
To tie the knot of wedded fate,
His last bid, desolate and late.
Her world was full, complete, content,
Their love's sad echo, now silent, spent.
This saga of lovers intertwined,
Sung in whispers by the winds of time.
Two hearts entwined, yet lived apart,
Each a mirror to the other's heart.
Love can birth from pain and sorrow,
A tiny spark of a brighter tomorrow.
Yet within each hope and second chance,
Lies the poignant essence of life's romance.

Love Happens In Pieces

See Through The Agony

In the carnage of our love's sudden demise,
Upon the crumpled letters of promised lies,
Bleakly stares a bare heart, devoid of guise,
Where love was once effulgent, a bitter ache now lies.
From this winter's heartbreak, no leaf could unfurl,
The grim echo of words, harsh as steel on pearl,
Echoes through the bare hallways of my world,
As our sacred ballet dissolves into a hurtful twirl.
Dreams of star-crossed journeys and sunlit smiles,
A lie dissolved in the murky tears of our trials,
For love is a distant moon, treacherous with guile,
In its crescent cradle, dwells the echo of goodbyes.
Your shadow lingers still, ghostly as the moonlight's caress,
In the recesses of my thoughts, love undressed,
Poignant silhouettes in an endless game of chess,

Only silence resides, in the ruins of our distress.
Broken chords and discordant notes I glean,
On the silenced piano of love's obliterated scene,
Lost are we now, within an ethereal sheen,
Ever fading into a nocturne of a forgotten dream.
What we had once was splendid and keen,
In aftermath it's but a hollow, remorseful scream.
Crying against the storm of sorrow's reign,
A tragic opus echoes in our love's lost theme.
Where once was us, now just memory's stain,
A fleeting passion caught in time's disdain,
Embers cool beneath the moon's cold reign,
Where our love once blossomed, only pain now reigns.
This, the wreckage of hearts asunder,
Drowning in a rainstorm of shattered wonder,
Witness of the breakage, aftermath's plunder,
In a play once sweet, now a somber thunder.
Oh, tragic artistry of the broken heart's pique,
Within the shards, the bitter-sweet reek,
Of love departed, once vivid, now bleak,

This is the canvas of the aftermath, of an ugly breakup's peak.

The Heart And Soul Merges To Find The Betrayal

A Pinch In The Soul

Splinters of love scattered across my soul,

A darkened sun weeps where our laughter used to roll.

Reflections in tears once diamonds of the heart,

Now mere shards of a canvas torn apart.

Whispered promises left abandoned in the wind,

Stanzas of love turned thorny and singed.

Like forgotten verses, the stories of us fade,

Washed away by time's relentless cascade.

Love's fragrant garden lies in ruins, love's bloom withdrawn,

Fires of passion, frozen, love's music forever gone.

Each tender word, each gentle touch, exiled into the night,

Where once bloomed orchards of affection, now stand ruins of spite.

Amid the wreckage of sweet yesterdays, under heartache's smoky pall,

Our voices echo faintly against memories crumbling wall.

In sorrow's frigid chambers, the frostbite of the end,

Only solitaire whispers remain of a lover and a friend.

Night comes, uninvited, on a ship of shattered dreams,

And a requiem for us is sung by melancholy streams.

A tangled labyrinth of broken hopes we leave behind,

Shattered mirror of affection, reflecting the wreckage of two minds.

Beneath the remnants of the war that love and hate design,

A teardrop echoes the silent lullaby of goodbye.

Laying wreaths of solitude in love's once vibrant chapel,

Walking down the lanes of memories that became a battle.

Through the icy winter of heartbreak, there will rise a hopeful sun,

But the haunting phantom of 'we were' will never be undone.

Yes, it was an ugly parting, bitter fruits of love's retreat,

Yet, in every falling tear, the love and hate still meet.

From the broken statue of affection, may we rise, the heart rebuild,

Seek a refuge in forgiveness, in our hearts, the anger stilled.

We live in the aftermath, the echoes of the rupture,

A grim testament of time, love's cruel and ugly fracture.

Bitter Taste Of Love

The Roller Coaster Ride

Upon a tide of uncertainty, sailed a mother and her pride,
Away from a country old, their past sorrows beside.
Single yet stronger than armies she seemed,
Fuelled by a dream, a mother's dream to be redeemed.
No lavish ships bore them, no crew sang their song,
Across the mighty ocean, where they'd belong.
Her hands nurtured hope, in the womb of the unknown,
Nurturing love's bud in this barren world, alone.
With a tiny heart clinging close to her breast,
She, an empress in exile, bound for a daunting quest.
A humble sphere cradling love's tender shrine,
Together, the map of their world they'd design.
Not for her, the aroma of ancestral lands,
New is her continent, shifting as the desert sands.
Under the aegis of distant stars they align,

Boundless, like their hearts entwined in time.
Her whispered lullabies in the moonlight dance,
Stories of brave knights, love's defiant stance.
Melting into the laughter of her cherubic joy,
Both playing with destiny like a coy, timeless toy.
Silver dawns break through the curtained night,
Upon a new landscape where she's to ignite,
Lighting lanterns of learning, undying hope, fierce love,
Echoing resilience beneath the heavens above.
Strength, unyielding, flows through her veins,
Turning struggles into verses, pains into refrains.
Bathing each dawn in courage, she, the sun anew,
In this land of plenty, writes their life in hues.
Under the maple and pine, she stands tall and firm,
Planting seeds of survival, let her child discern.
And under her shadow may this child learn,
To endure the storm and wait for his turn.
Amid the cool serenity of mountain caps snow-white,
Her eyes reflect stories of her resolute fight.
In this novel expanse, new roots, they begin to thrive,

From the ashes of past, rises a single mom's undying drive.

A symphony she crafts, from the fragments of the night,

Single but unbroken, in her child's heart ignites,

In the crevices of this distant continent, unfurl,

A new chapter of resilience, a mother's pearlescent world.

Masks That Cover The Heart

A Musk So Clear

In the silence of her solitude, unmarked by scorn,
Resides a damsel fair, by life's betrayals worn.
A gentle heart that once felt the bite of love's false hymn,
But yet a new dawn wakes, her story's stage not dim.
Held captive once by dreams of phantom arms and gaze,
An illusion's love she cherished in tender ways.
Whispered words of faith that twisted into deceit,
Caused her hopeful heart in passion's pulse to retreat.
In the darkest valley, cast in despair's shroud,
Through the echoes of her loneliness cried out loud.
Scorned by love's betrayal, feeling less, feeling marred,
Left in love's shadows, by deception scarred.
Then in love's winter, there bloomed a distant glow,
Softly it shimmered, like moonlight on virgin snow.
Her world colored by this mysterious hue,

She fell once again, but this love was fresh, new.

Treading softly, not to wake old hurt asleep,

She tasted love anew, a secret she'd keep.

In soft-spoken verses, in sighs amidst the trees,

She loved again, moved by love's mystic melodies.

Gone was the phantom of love's illusion grand,

In his place was a presence, true as sea and sand.

Her heart he stirred with genuine warmth, sweet and raw,

Fulfilling the dreams, even illusions never saw.

To love she surrenders, baring her unbroken core,

Embracing vulnerability, fearing no more.

Unhindered by yesterday's mischievous sprite,

In love's arena, she dances once again in delight.

Cheated, deceived, but stronger in her splendid design,

Her faith renewed, love's familiar touch now divine.

This time it's real, not a passing charade,

An authentically beautiful serenade.

This single woman, radiant as the evening star,

Her heart was wounded but it still dared to spar.

Loving again after being sorely mistreated,

Blessed by the promise, that love won't be defeated.

For even from betrayal's relentless affray,

Springs the opportunity for a brighter day.

Now here stands a woman, bathed in love's warmest glow,

Heart on her sleeve, free of fear, love's sweet tableau.

Springing Love For Another Time

Love Hails From West

In the heart of British soil, down Woking way,

A single-mum resided, love lost along the fray.

Young Bella, in her prime, beneath winter's silent bough,

Raising wee Emma single-handedly, mastering her how.

Through school runs and soft smiles, skinned knees, and tears,

Sole warrior in the battlefield of toddler years.

Fending for her lass, she harboured quiet hope,

In dreams beneath the pillow, helped her lonely heart to cope.

A tale of love undaunted, hidden in her eyes,

Where melancholy melted 'neath the glow of golden skies.

Behind a careworn visage, wore like an honoured badge,

Lay an untouched heart that echoed longing's silent adage.

Of whispers in the twilight, promises kept untold,

Tales of true romance and courting ways of old.

For though she's cast as a heroine, toughened by the winds,

Bella dreams of chivalry, of tender-hearted friends.

Then upon one cold December, misty winter's morn,

A handsome stranger arrived, love's harbinger reborn.

Aptly named Edmund, his aura full of charm,

Melting Bella's heart and quieting her qualm.

Cascading rivers of laughter, intertwining tales and toasts,

The Christmas air hummed, full of wandering ghosts.

Eyes sparking like fireworks in Guy Fawkes' ebony night,

There was warmth in their meeting, the dawning of the light.

Drawn to Bella's radiance, Edmund saw her through,

Beyond the drab apparel, to the gem of value true.

Through tangled webs of duties, they weaved their time, made space,

In Edmund's eyes, Bella bloomed, a flower with silent grace.

Their souls enmeshed like tendrils, tangled in Love's eternal quest,

Caught in whispers of night, laying fears to rest.

A toast to unseen futures, intertwined as vine and branch,

Daring to believe, love was no chance, but the purposeful dance.

Her world that once was grey, coloured with desire,

Her soul a lit fireplace, fed by passion's fire.

A protective bear he was, in love with Bella and her cub,

A beacon in their lives, filling gaps in the drab.

He wooed with verse and sonnet, Love's letters old and true,

Where prose sparked feelings dormant, turning the greyest blue.

He looked beyond her exterior, saw the depths within her soul,

Embracing Bella wholly, he made her again feel whole.

Fleeting moments etched in amber, turning pages of time,

Their journey of becoming, Bella's fairy-tale rhyme.

Beneath the prying eyes of stars, in secret lovers' whispers,

The bond between two souls grew, tearing down resistors.

Their love story unveiled in gentle daylight's smile,

Transcending their challenges, life's obstacle-filled aisle.

And so, the tale unfolded of a love deeply kind,

An extraordinary man, a single-mum's fervent find.

Their saga carries forth, a chronicle rich and real,

Full of undying love, a potent antidote to heal.

Where destiny ties knots, may the tapestry unwind,

True love discovered in twilight's bind, and dreams left behind.

Love Is Warm

A Love To Be Loved

In the land of amour, baguettes, and wine,
Resided an Indian mom, with spirit so divine,
Anaya was her name, poised with charms bright,
In the heart of Paris, under the starry night.
Five thousand miles from her native land,
Fighting life's storms with a steady hand.
One son, her heart, her life, her hope,
Held close by the ties of love's unending rope.
Worn, yet beautiful, she stands alone,
Eyes like mystery, in their depths untold.
Nights spent in silence, drowned in tears,
Living through struggles, yet suppressing her fears.
Morning awakens in a ballet of colors,
As she embraces the dawn, her solitude unfurls.
Work calls to her, in silence, she steers,
Through lanes and bylanes, shedding unseen tears.

A new day in France, another bout to face,
Challenging, fierce, yet full of grace.
Every dawn bringing fresh hopes to feed,
Every dusk retelling stories of unspoken deed.
Across a café's soft, enchanting hue,
Appeared a stranger, with eyes of smoky blue.
Adrian, they called him, a sculptor by trade,
Gentle in manners, in Parisian elegance draped.
Strangers no longer, love then did weave,
Between their hearts, a tale of reprieve.
Adrian's chiseled hands held her sorrows,
Unraveling her essence, waking brighter tomorrows.
Her son found solace in Adrian's smile,
Found a father figure in him, free of guile.
Adrian and Anaya, a seamless blend,
Bound by love, a message they send.
Beneath the sky, jeweled with stardust,
In this city of love, their hearts thus entrust.
Amidst moonlight whispers and heartfelt promises,
A new love story emerges, past the abysses.

Her roots in India, blossoms in France,
In this symphony of love, her spirit danced.
They dared to dream, dared to weave,
A story of love, you've got to believe.
In shadows and light, in joys and in sorrow,
In todays and tomorrows, love continued to borrow.
Pieces of her heart, bits of his soul,
Together they found a love beautifully whole.
Anaya, the Indian single mom, discovered more than love,
In a stranger from France, under stars above.
For love not just mended her broken heart,
But also offered her life a brand-new start.
Thus is the tale of love, in myriad hues,
In the heart of France, amidst mornings' dew.
An Indian mother, a Parisian gentleman,
Their story sings on, beyond time's span.
Five thousand words could never tell,
The depth of love, in their hearts that dwell.
An Indian single mom, her tale unfurls,

In the city of love, where her new life swirls.

Heavens Drool For The Heart

Love Is Like A Poem

Upon the Ganges' distant shore she dreamed,
Of lights and artistry that danced in a realm unseen,
A daughter of India, in Paris, she blossomed,
Single mother, independent and full of wisdom.
Jasmine veiled streets remembered and replaced,
With the quaint aroma of French pastries laced,
Leaving her native home and cherished soil,
In search of dreams, in new land she began to toil.
Unyielding as the river in monsoon tide,
Bold and brave with love at her side,
Bore the weight of her past, embraced her present,
Strong roots bore a blossom ever so resplendent.
A child she cradled, her heart's treasure,
Soft brown eyes mirrored her own measure,
Young enough to cherish fairy tales and pixie dust,
In the land of Voltaire, her trust she thrust.

As she stitched tales of Rama and Krishna,
Into dreams of Quasimodo in Fantasia,
With strokes of henna on the Seine's sighing heart,
She painted love, with colours from Matisse's cart.
Her radiant warmth set Paris alight,
Even the moon whispered tales of her starry night,
Every lullaby spun tales of a princess and her knight,
Where their love endured despite their plight.
Amidst daily hustles and subtle hints of fate,
Her heart found whispers of an unknown mate,
Eyes blue as lapis met brown in serendipity's great design,
Where two souls connected, in love so divine.
Chai simmered with notes of coffee on rainy nights,
Words swirled into verses as day met twilight,
Passions merged, traditions twined in fervent dance,
Two hearts stitched together in a cosmic trance.
Binds of the past met bridges of the future,
Her heart stitched a beautiful sutra,

Of an Indian damsel in the city of romance,
Savoring love, dancing in trance.
Daughter's laughter echoed around the Eiffel Tower,
Petals of love bloomed, moments began to flower,
Echoing melodies of love sang across the Seine,
Life in harmony, an intricate love's refrain.
As she told tales of her childhood yore,
He found poetry in the heart he yearned to adore,
Her love swept him into a melodic dance,
An Indian lullaby in the heart of France.
For her journey's not of thorns or pity's tales,
Her life – an artistry, an exotic sales,
An Indian Single-mom, a Phoenix's ascension,
Loving, thriving in the City of Passion.
Together they watched their dreams unfurl,
A resilient single mother, now loved by her French Earl,
To a Parisian sunrise they sang in loving tone,
Love knew no borders, for it had found a home.

To life, to love, she sang with flair,
A tale of hope from the heart of an Indian solitaire,
Woven into verses five thousand words strong,
An epic poem of love where two souls belong.
This, a saga of a mother's devotion,
Painting love on a transcontinental potion,
Under the glowing hues of the setting sun,
Her tale of love had only just begun.

About the Author

Debanjali Nag, the author is a Marketing Manager who possesses in-depth expertise in generating influential thought leadership and PR content, and orchestrating holistic marketing strategies. Her proficiency lies in managing multi-platform campaigns, interpreting analytics, and conducting market research, with an established track record of bolstering brand image, augmenting customer engagement, and amplifying revenue. With outstanding skills in teamwork and communication, the author endeavors to stimulate growth and enhancement for any organization they become a part of. Having published 3 books of her own, she has penned 35+ anthologies till date with Ukiyoto Publishers. She has her Hindi Poetry Book 'Shikasta Qalb' by an Indian Publishing House. Since 2021, she started as an open-mic performer across India as well out of her passion to connect with people from all across the country.

www.ingramcontent.com/pod-product-compliance
Lightning Source LLC
LaVergne TN
LVHW041636070526
838199LV00052B/3400